UNLEASH YOUR LEADERSHIP POTENTIAL

Navigating Your Leadership Journey with Confidence

By

Debra J. Price

Table of Content

Introduction

In a world where leadership transcends titles and extends into the very fabric of our actions, "Unleash Your Leadership Potential" embarks on a journey to uncover the hidden brilliance within each of us. This book is your guide to navigating the realms of leadership, revealing the latent capabilities that can transform you into a catalyst for positive change and lasting impact.

Leadership, often obscured by misconceptions and stereotypes, is not a privilege reserved for a select few. Instead, it's an innate quality that dwells within everyone, waiting to be awakened and harnessed. Whether you're at the helm of a team, an entrepreneur charting your course, or an individual looking to lead your life with purpose, this book offers insights that transcend traditional notions of leadership.

Here, we'll traverse the intricate landscapes of self-awareness, effective communication, empathetic leadership, and continuous growth. Through the pages of this book, you'll embark on a journey of self-discovery, learning to recognize the unique qualities that define your leadership style and influence. You'll explore the power of authenticity, resilience, and adaptability in the face of challenges.

As we delve deeper, you'll uncover strategies to nurture your potential, embracing a growth mindset that paves the way for personal and professional transformation. We'll also delve into the profound art of empowering and inspiring others, understanding that authentic leadership involves elevating those around you.

"Unleash Your Leadership Potential" is not just a book—it's an invitation to embark on a journey of empowerment, self-discovery, and leadership excellence. Together, we'll peel back the layers that shroud your hidden brilliance, illuminating a path that leads to impactful leadership and a legacy of positive change. As you turn the pages, remember that your leadership journey is unique, and your potential is waiting to be unleashed upon the world.

Chapter 1

Finding the Hidden Leader Within

Leadership, a beacon that has led humanity's progress throughout history, is frequently regarded to be a quality reserved for charismatic leaders at the top of society. This image, however, ignores an important fact: leadership is not limited to individuals in positions of formal power. It is within each person, waiting to be awakened and harnessed. This chapter, "Discovering the Hidden Leader Within," takes us on a journey to discover the latent leadership potential that we all possess.

Recognizing Your Leadership Potential

A profound insight into oneself is at the heart of every great leader. Recognizing leadership potential in yourself necessitates a shift in perspective—a recognition that leadership is a dynamic attribute that can be nurtured in anyone ready to study and develop it.

Leadership isn't just about making big decisions or capturing people's attention. It includes a variety of big and minor qualities and acts that affect and inspire those around you. Leading a team, completing a project, and listening to others are all examples of leadership. It is critical to recognize that leadership can take many forms, independent of titles or positions.

Reflect on times when you took the initiative, displayed resilience, or positively influenced others to realize your leadership potential. By recognizing these occasions, you can begin to unravel the leadership threads woven throughout your life. This self-awareness serves as the cornerstone for your leadership path.

Understanding the Hidden Leadership Concept

Hidden leadership defies traditional wisdom by emphasizing that leadership is not simply defined by visibility or charisma. It recognizes that profound leadership is often found in the quieter corners of a team or organization—individuals who lead through cooperation, empathy, and a strong commitment to progress.

These unseen leaders may not be visible, yet they are the driving factors behind successful undertakings. They have attributes such as honesty, humility, and a genuine commitment to a cause. Their leadership is distinguished by a focus on the greater good rather than personal recognition.

Understanding the concept of hidden leadership enables you to rethink leadership in light of your unique abilities and principles. It encourages you to think of leadership as a web of interwoven deeds rather than a single flash of fame. By doing so, you accept the idea that leadership is a varied path that people of diverse backgrounds and temperaments can explore and hone.

Investigating the Factors That May Have Kept Your Leadership Qualities Hidden

As you go deeper into uncovering your latent leadership potential, it's critical to tackle the factors that may have concealed these characteristics from your consciousness. Among these elements are societal expectations, prior experiences, and personal misgivings, all of which contribute to a self-imposed limitation of your leadership capacity.

Certain preconceptions about leaders are frequently perpetuated throughout society. The image of a leader is typically outgoing, confident, and assertive. However, these characteristics do not encompass the entire range of leadership skills. If you identify more as an introvert or have different strengths, that doesn't imply you don't have leadership potential. Introverts, in reality, can demonstrate great leadership skills such as active listening, empathy, and strategic thinking.

Past events might also play an important role in concealing your leadership qualities. A perceived failure or a situation in which your thoughts were not acknowledged may have resulted in self-doubt. These events build over time, producing barriers that limit your readiness to assume leadership roles.

Personal misgivings, which are typically caused by comparisons with others or a fear of failure, can also contribute to your unwillingness to identify and accept your leadership potential.

This chapter invites you to investigate and dismantle these impediments. You can transcend societal expectations, prior experiences, and internal uncertainties that have hampered your leadership journey by identifying them. This self-awareness allows you to let go of limiting ideas, build self-confidence, and develop a more accurate story about your potential.

It also establishes the foundation for your transforming journey. By recognizing your leadership potential, you accept that leadership is available to everyone.

Understanding the concept of hidden leadership enables you to reinvent leadership on your terms, breaking free from stereotypical roles. Finally, by investigating the causes that may have kept your leadership qualities hidden, you begin the process of removing these obstacles and revealing the leader within.

Finally, leadership is not a faraway goal; it is a journey that begins within. It is about embracing your unique abilities, valuing different types of leadership, and recognizing that your experiences, no matter how large or small, contribute to your progress as a leader. Your leadership journey is only getting started, and by revealing the hidden leader within, you are laying the groundwork for a great transformation.

Chapter 2

Accepting Your Leadership Potential

Leadership is a journey, not a destination, that weaves its way through the tapestry of your life. In this chapter, "Accepting your leadership potential," we explore the deep revelation that leadership isn't about adhering to prescribed positions; it's about recognizing and developing the leader within you, in all facets of your life.

Uncovering Your Leadership Journey
Each of us has a unique leadership journey that has been influenced by our experiences, values, and objectives. Your

journey may include career pursuits, personal connections, and community involvement. This path necessitates reflection and a desire to delve into the depths of your past and present.

Begin by exploring the leadership threads that run through your life. Consider times when you stepped up to help, encourage, or inspire others. These incidents may not have been spectacular or significant, but they are the seeds that will blossom your leadership journey.

Understanding your path entails recognizing the struggles you've faced, the lessons you've learned, and the growth you've experienced. You create a narrative that is distinctively yours by weaving these pieces together—a narrative that represents your changing identity as a leader.

Getting Over Self-Doubt and Imposter Syndrome

Accepting your leadership destiny necessitates facing one of the most formidable obstacles: self-doubt. The insidious voice whispering questions about your competence, known as imposter syndrome, can cast a pall over your leadership potential. But keep in mind that imposter syndrome is a projection of your inner critic, not reality.

The first step in overcoming self-doubt is admitting that it exists. Recognize that even the most accomplished leaders have experienced times of doubt. You gain perspective and empowerment by identifying imposter syndrome as a typical struggle.

Self-compassion should take the place of self-doubt. Treat yourself with the same compassion and understanding that you would extend to a friend experiencing similar doubts. Accept your flaws as necessary components of your development. Seek mentors, role models, and supportive groups to remind you of your skills and to celebrate your accomplishments.

Accepting Your Role as a Leader in Different Aspects of Life

Leadership is not limited to the boardroom or official positions; it pervades all aspects of life. Leadership influences everything from your relationships with coworkers to your contributions to your family, community, and even personal hobbies.

Accept your leadership destiny by recognizing your ability to lead in both large and minor ways. It may entail promoting teamwork, engaging team members, and driving initiatives in your business. It could mean becoming a source of direction, support, and inspiration for your loved ones in your own life.

By embracing leadership in a variety of contexts, you broaden your awareness of its subtleties. This holistic approach expands your leadership capability since the abilities you gain in one setting frequently have a favorable impact on another. Leading with authenticity and empathy in your relationships can improve your professional leadership effectiveness, and vice versa.

I encourage you to start on a self-discovery and empowerment journey. Recognize the occasions that have shaped you as a leader to reveal your unique leadership journey. Replace self-doubt with self-compassion and a growth attitude to overcome the self-doubt that wants to limit your potential. Finally, accept your job as a leader in all facets of your life, knowing that your leadership destiny is not restricted by circumstance.

Your leadership path is as varied as your experiences. It's a fabric made up of your abilities, growth, and connections. By accepting your destiny as a leader, you not only improve your own life but also brighten the route for others to follow. You are not merely a victim of fate; you are the architect of it.

Chapter 3

Unleashing Your Leadership Identity

The route of become a powerful leader is a tour of self-discovery, authenticity, and alignment. "Unleashing Your Leadership Identity," the heart of your transformative journey, goes into the deep process of recognizing who you are as a leader and how you may channel your uniqueness into a force that inspires and directs others.

Identifying Your Leadership Style and Strengths

Every leader has a distinct style—a distinctive blend of attributes, tactics, and techniques that determine their interactions and influence. Identifying your leadership style is a critical step in understanding your leadership personality.

Begin by meditating on your natural tendencies, preferences, and habits when leading others. Are you a visionary, motivating people with your big-picture thinking? Are you a collaborator, building good ties inside teams? Perhaps you're a strategic thinker, continually recognizing opportunities for growth and advancement.

Simultaneously, recognize your strengths—the qualities that set you different and empower you to make a positive influence. These could range from great communication abilities to a penchant for problem-solving or a remarkable capacity to remain calm under pressure.

By recognizing your leadership style and talents, you can customize your approach to different situations and capitalize on your intrinsic advantages. This self-awareness offers the foundation upon which your leadership identity will thrive.

Nurturing Authenticity and Integrity in Leadership

Authenticity is the cornerstone of good leadership. It's about connecting your actions, words, and objectives with your true self. Authentic leaders are real, truthful, and unafraid to display weakness. They acquire trust and respect by being honest with themselves and embracing their shortcomings.

Nurturing authenticity demands embracing your uniqueness without fear of condemnation. It's about being comfortable in your skin and bringing your complete self to your leadership roles. Embrace your strengths, acknowledge your flaws, and allow your actual character to come through.

Integrity is the partner of sincerity. It's the commitment to ethical behavior and honesty, especially when faced with adversities. Leaders who uphold their beliefs and display integrity motivate their teams to do the same. When your behaviors constantly coincide with your values, you develop a foundation of trust that strengthens your leadership impact.

Aligning Your Values with Your Leadership Approach

Leadership without values is directionless; it lacks the moral compass that governs decisions and actions. Aligning your beliefs with your leadership strategy is the essence of ethical, purpose-driven leadership.

Begin by establishing your core values—the principles that define who you are and what you stand for. These values are the foundation around which your leadership identity is created. Once you've defined your values, integrate them into your leadership strategy. Consider how they inform your decisions, interactions, and the culture you establish within your team or community.

When values guide your leadership, you not only navigate obstacles with integrity but also establish an environment where people can grow. Your staff acknowledges your constancy and genuineness, establishing a culture of trust and collaboration.

Identifying your leadership style and talents helps you to harness your natural abilities for maximum impact. Nurturing honesty and integrity sets the tone for meaningful connections and trust-building. Finally, combining your values with your leadership strategy guarantees that your leadership path is founded on purpose and ethics.

Unleashing your leadership identity is not about emulating others or adhering to expectations; it's about recognizing your unique constellation of talents, values, and experiences. As you embark on this journey, you not only become a more effective leader but also inspire others to embrace their authenticity and lead from the heart. Your leadership identity is a gift to your team, your organization, and the world around you.

Chapter 4

Characteristics of Effective Leadership

Leadership is a delicate dance of traits, actions, and attitudes that form the way you influence and inspire those around you. In "Characteristics of Effective Leadership," we look into the basic traits and qualities that distinguish impactful leaders. This chapter acts as a compass, directing you toward establishing a holistic understanding of leadership effectiveness and applying these traits to your leadership path.

Exploring Key Traits and Qualities of Successful Leaders

Effective leadership is not primarily characterized by one's ability to command attention or give orders. It is a complex blend of attributes that equip leaders to connect, motivate, and direct their teams. These attributes extend beyond titles or positions, showing in deeds that create a lasting influence.

One such attribute is empathy—an crucial cornerstone of leadership. Empathetic leaders comprehend the needs, feelings, and viewpoints of those they lead. This understanding creates the cornerstone of healthy relationships and efficient communication.

Adaptability is another key attribute. The capacity to navigate change and uncertainty with resilience enables leaders to direct their teams through problems. A growth mentality complements adaptation, encouraging leaders to consider setbacks as opportunities for learning and advancement.

Visionary thinking, the ability to see beyond the present and design a course for the future, separates extraordinary leaders. By creating a clear vision, leaders inspire commitment and align efforts toward common goals.

Developing a Holistic Understanding of Leadership Effectiveness

Leadership effectiveness is a broad term, and it's not tied to a particular strategy or collection of attributes. It's about knowing that good leadership is a fluid, dynamic journey affected by circumstances and the people you lead.

To establish a holistic knowledge of leadership success, it's crucial to appreciate that no leader exemplifies every trait flawlessly. Instead, focus on accepting your strengths and fostering areas for growth. Effective leaders are self-aware, identifying where they thrive and where they may develop.

Another facet of holistic leadership is realizing that leadership extends beyond the bounds of an organization or team. Effective leaders affect not only the present but also the future. Their deeds ripple through the lives of those they lead, leaving a legacy of positive transformation.

Applying These Characteristics to Your Hidden Leadership Journey

As a covert leader, your impact may not always be immediately obvious, but it is substantial nonetheless. Applying the traits of effective leadership to your journey means harnessing your abilities to generate a ripple of influence in your interactions, undertakings, and initiatives.

Begin by examining your present strengths and areas for growth. Consider how your particular blend of qualities connects with the essential elements of effective leadership. This evaluation gives a plan for your growth and development as a leader.

Embrace empathy as you traverse your hidden leadership journey. Understand the needs and aspirations of others around you, and build meaningful connections. Lead with honesty, allowing your principles and integrity to come through in every action.

Adaptability is extremely crucial to leaders since your ability to adjust to changing events and obstacles influences your impact. By keeping open to new ideas and techniques, you build an environment of continual improvement.

Develop a strong vision for your hidden leadership path. Even in smaller areas, having a sense of purpose and direction informs your activities and encourages others you connect with.

This chapter is a deep dive into the basic attributes that make leaders effective. These attributes create the foundation upon which impactful leadership is constructed. By investigating and understanding these attributes, you receive insights into your own strengths and growth areas.

Remember that leadership effectiveness is not about conforming to a fixed pattern. It's about embracing your uniqueness, having a growth mentality, and fostering meaningful connections. As a leader, your impact may be discreet, yet it is far-reaching. By applying these characteristics to your path, you create leadership that uplifts, inspires, and leaves a lasting legacy of good change. Your leadership is not tied to a single moment; it's a continuum of acts that influence the world around you.

Chapter 5

Mastering Self-Leadership

In the broad fabric of leadership, one thread stands out as indispensable—self-leadership. This chapter, "Mastering Self-Leadership," goes into the crucial skill of understanding and directing oneself before guiding others. It analyzes how fostering self-awareness, creating objectives, and practicing self-care and resilience are crucial in nurturing leadership excellence.

Cultivating Self-Awareness for Effective Leadership

At the basis of effective leadership lies self-awareness—a thorough grasp of your thoughts, feelings, strengths, and areas for progress. Self-aware leaders are alert to their reactions, prejudices, and triggers, allowing them to respond rather than react. This awareness extends to how they affect individuals around them.

To cultivate self-awareness, start on a voyage of introspection. Regularly analyze your ideas and feelings, especially during challenging times. Seek comments from trusted peers or mentors to gain insights into your blind spots. This process of self-discovery offers the foundation for real and powerful leadership.

A self-aware leader acknowledges their limitations and is unafraid to accept help or delegate work when necessary. This humility encourages a culture of collaboration and ongoing growth among your team or community.

Setting Goals and Managing Your Personal Growth

Leadership is a path of continual progress, and setting goals is the compass that leads this trip. Effective leaders set goals that are not only outcome-driven but also focused on personal development. These goals act as stepping stones to realizing your potential as a leader.

Begin by creating clear, measurable objectives that match your vision of leadership greatness. Break these objectives into small steps, providing a roadmap for your advancement. Regularly monitor your progress and change your goals as needed to ensure you stay on track.

Setting goals not only propels you toward your leadership vision but also indicates your commitment to the ongoing improvement of the people you lead. It generates a culture of learning, inspiring people to invest in their progress.

Practicing Self-Care and Resilience to Sustain Leadership Excellence

Leadership may be hard, and the route to unlocking untapped leadership potential involves resilience and self-care. Leaders who disregard their well-being risk burnout and lost effectiveness.

Practicing self-care means prioritizing your physical, emotional, and mental well-being. Ensure you receive appropriate rest, engage in activities that refresh you, and handle stress through strategies like mindfulness or meditation. Prioritize time for hobbies and activities that bring you joy, as they add to your general well-being.

Resilience is the ability to bounce back from obstacles and disappointments. Leaders that exercise resilience regard barriers as opportunities for progress. Develop a mindset that reframes failures as learning experiences. Resilient leaders also develop a support network of mentors, peers, and friends who provide encouragement and assistance during stressful times.

Incorporate self-care and resilience strategies into your routine to sustain your leadership journey. By taking care of yourself, you model the significance of well-being to the people you lead. Your ability to manage your issues creates confidence in your leadership and encourages others to adopt similar methods.

In summary, by increasing self-awareness, you establish the foundation for real leadership that connects with others. Setting goals and controlling personal growth moves you forward on your leadership journey, displaying your dedication to continual improvement. Practicing self-care and resilience not only supports your effectiveness but also sets an example for people under your influence.

Remember, the journey of leadership begins within. As you master self-leadership, you equip yourself with the tools needed to assist others effectively. A self-aware, goal-driven, and resilient leader leads by example, inspiring their team to embrace growth, well-being, and the pursuit of greatness. Your mastery of self-leadership ensures that your leadership path is not just impactful but also sustainable and fulfilling.

Chapter 6

Communication the Key to Influential Leadership

In the world of leadership, communication acts as a link between inspiration and implementation, as well as between vision and action. This chapter's main topic, "Communication: The Key to Influential Leadership," explores the nuances of effective communication. To motivate and inspire the people you lead, it examines the art of improving communication skills, the value of active listening, as well as the power of empathy.

Developing Skillful Communication

The ability to effectively communicate thoughts, ideas, and visions to others is essential for effective leadership. Effective communication involves more than just conveying information; it also entails developing a language that engages and persuades.

Clarity is a good place to start. It is possible to reduce complicated ideas to easily comprehensible phrases. Avoid using technical terms or jargon that could turn off your readers.

Exercise restraint. Clear communication grabs attention and has an impact that lasts. The main point should not be diluted by verbosity or tangents.

To reach your audience, adjust your communication approach. Think about your listeners' tastes, history, and needs. To make sure your message is received well, modify your wording and strategy.

Active and Empathetic Listening

Speaking is an essential part of communication, but listening is just as important—if not more so—than speaking. Genuine connections and a trusting environment are built on active and empathic listening.

Engaging with the speaker fully is part of active listening. Maintain eye contact, convey attention nonverbally, and keep distractions to a minimum. To be sure you understand what you've heard, repeat it back.

Listening with empathy goes beyond mere comprehension. It requires paying attention to the speaker's feelings and viewpoints. Look beyond the words to comprehend the underlying emotions and purposes.

You may affirm the experiences of those you lead by engaging in active and empathic listening. This encourages open communication and cultivates a climate of respect.

Creating Compelling Narratives to Inspire and Motivate People's

Stories have a special ability to capture people's attention. Leaders employ the ability to develop captivating narratives to paint visions, motivate action, and establish a feeling of purpose.

Recognize your audience before anything else. Make your story relevant to their interests, values, and goals. The narrative should make sense in the context of the audience, whether it is a team, a boardroom, or a community.

Create a compelling narrative arc. Introduce a problem or dispute, describe the steps taken to solve it, and then offer a gratifying solution or a promising outlook for the future.

Add some emotion to your story. What makes a story memorable and powerful is emotion. Whether it's arousal, empathetic response, or inspiration, emotional resonance makes sure that your message sticks with listeners long after it's been said.

Gaining strong communication skills enables you to express your views concisely and clearly. Listening that is engaged and empathic strengthens relationships and builds trust. Your visions become stories that arouse inspiration and drive motivation when you create appealing storylines.

Speaking and listening must be balanced carefully to have an effective conversation. By developing this skill, you build a connection between the hearts of those you lead and your leadership principles.

Keep in mind that communication involves more than just words; it also involves your presence, your nonverbal indications, and the feelings you arouse. Effective communicators engage, persuade, and inspire in addition to informing. Your capacity for building relationships through communication increases the impact of your leadership and creates a lasting impression on people who take your lead.

Chapter 7

Using Emotional Intelligence and Empathy to Lead

Technical proficiency and strategic thinking are crucial in the field of leadership, but emotional intelligence and empathy are the keys to effective leadership. We will look at the enormous influence these traits have on leadership. Investigates the value of empathy, the development of emotional intelligence for decision-making, the skill of forging close bonds, and promoting team cohesion.

Knowing the Function of Empathy in Leadership

The basis of human connection, empathy serves as a link between differing viewpoints, experiences, and emotions. Empathy in leadership is essential for comprehending, inspiring, and directing individuals who are under your sway.

Empathetic leaders are aware of the diversity within their teams. They value the variety of backgrounds, difficulties, and goals that each person brings to their path.

Empathetic leaders actively listen to people and try to comprehend their feelings and points of view. They put themselves in other people's situations, promoting a sense of community and trust among the team members.

Empathy entails acting proactively to help and uplift; it goes beyond merely sympathizing with problems. It involves fostering a culture where team members are respected, listened to, and understood.

How to Develop Emotional Intelligence for Better Decision MakingMaking

The capacity to perceive, comprehend, control, and use your own emotions as well as the emotions of others is known as emotional intelligence. It serves as a crucial tool for leaders, directing their interactions, choices, and connections.

Understanding your emotional triggers, prejudices, and reactions is the first step in developing emotional intelligence. This knowledge gives you the power to respond in trying circumstances as opposed to simply reacting.

Effective emotional management is a trait of leaders, especially when under pressure. They are aware that how they react influences how the team will react.

Another aspect of emotional intelligence is the ability to recognize others' emotional states. Leaders are better able to offer the proper support and direction when they can recognize and sympathize with the emotions of their team members.

Creating enduring connections and promoting team cohesion

More than just assigning duties and giving instructions, leadership involves fostering connections and assembling a cohesive team. Connecting on a personal level, acting authentically, and building a feeling of community are all necessary for developing strong connections.

Leadership styles that place a high value on relationships are characterized by open and honest communication. They promote discussion, offer criticism, and are attentive to suggestions and issues.

Genuineness fosters trust. Team members feel more at ease sharing their struggles and concerns when their leaders exhibit vulnerability. This openness promotes respect and cooperation between parties.

Recognizing each person's abilities and contributions is necessary to promote team cohesion. Tasks that are appropriate for team members' skills are assigned by emotionally intelligent leaders, which improves performance and raises morale.

Deepening your awareness of others via empathy promotes an atmosphere of trust, inclusivity, and support. You can manage complex emotions, make wise judgments, and create harmonious relationships if you have emotional intelligence.

Empathy and emotional intelligence are not merely skills to be learned; they are an attitude that permeates your leadership style. You can go beyond being a mere manager by appreciating and comprehending the human side of leadership and develop into an inspiring figure.

Keep in mind that leadership is about the people who work to attain goals, not just the goals themselves. The success of your leadership journey is ensured by your capacity to lead with empathy and emotional intelligence, which also makes it meaningful and inspiring for others who follow your lead.

Chapter 8

Navigating Difficulties and Adversity

Adversity and challenges encountered along the path to leadership aren't things to avoid but rather present chances for development, education, and transformation. The focus of this chapter, "Navigating Difficulties and Adversity," explores the skill of embracing ambiguity, using problem-solving techniques in challenging circumstances, and learning insightful insights to enhance your leadership journey.

Embracing Change and Uncertainty as a Leader

Change and leadership are inextricably linked. Change is a continuous companion on the leadership journey, whether it is fueled by internal considerations or external forces. A change in perspective is necessary to embrace uncertainty; one that sees change not as a disruption but as a driver of creativity and advancement.

Your team's perception of and reaction to change is influenced by how well you as a leader handle uncertainty. Approach change transparently and openly. Explain the changes' justifications and expected advantages in detail. Recognize any difficulties or worries, but also draw attention to any potential advantages.

Include your staff in the process to give them the confidence to accept change. Ask for their opinions, suggestions, and feedback. This encourages a sense of ownership while also bringing different viewpoints to the table, which results in better decisions.

Strategies for Solving Problems in Complex Situations

Leaders are frequently required to handle complex problems that necessitate original solutions. Impactful leadership is characterized by effective problem-solving. It necessitates a fusion of analytical reasoning, creativity, and teamwork.

Start by dividing the challenge into smaller, more manageable parts. Examine the underlying causes and influencing elements of the problem. You may concentrate your efforts on the most important factors thanks to this clarity.

Encourage group collaboration while tackling problems. Utilize the varied viewpoints and abilities of your team members. Together, come up with answers, fostering a culture where everyone's opinion is respected.

Think about adopting a growth mentality, which sees obstacles as chances to grow and learn. This way of thinking enables you to see failures as opportunities for progress rather than obstacles.

Extracting Knowledge and Moving Forward from Obstacles

Challenges are not failures; rather, they are milestones on your path to leadership. Reflecting, learning, and incorporating discovered insights into your leadership style are all necessary steps in drawing lessons from adversities.

After overcoming a hurdle, pause to consider what went well and what may have been done better. Analyze the choices you made, the tactics you used, and the results that followed.

Ask your team and colleagues for comments. Their viewpoints can offer insightful information that you might have overlooked. You can use this criticism to direct your future decision- and problem-solving-making.

Adopt a philosophy of ongoing development. Every obstacle you conquer helps you become a better leader. Refine your strategy using the lessons you've learned to become better at addressing difficulties in the future.

Embracing change and uncertainty gives you the ability to lead with assurance and adaptability, motivating your team to take on problems head-on.

You can analyze complex problems with the help of problem-solving techniques, which encourage creative solutions that advance the cause. By drawing lessons from difficulties, you can turn obstacles into chances for improvement, establishing yourself as a strong and visionary leader.

Keep in mind that difficulties are milestones rather than obstacles on your path to leadership. Every obstacle you overcome helps you hone your abilities, expand your knowledge, and improve your capacity to lead with insight and assurance. By overcoming obstacles, you not only increase your leadership influence but also encourage people around you to face difficulty with fortitude and resiliency.

Chapter 9

Locating Your Inspirational Source

Inspiration serves as the bright thread that connects your actions, choices, and influence in the complex mosaic of leadership. The main topic of this chapter, "Locating Your Inspiration Source" discusses the crucial value of knowing where your drive and motivation come from. It explores the significant relationship between inspiration and your leadership mission as well as the transforming impact of using inspiration to further your leadership journey.

Using Your Passion and Motivational Sources

Leadership is about more than just planning and direction; it's about the passion and zeal that motivate you to take action. The key to finding the flame that starts your leadership journey is to tap into your sources of inspiration and enthusiasm.

Consider what inspires and motivates you first. What causes, circumstances, or difficulties make your heart race? These are the hints that point you in the direction of your passions.

Investigate your values and views. Your sense of purpose and commitment is increased when you focus your leadership efforts on the issues that are most important to you.

Find mentors or role models who inspire you. Their experiences can shed light on how they turned passion into effective leadership.

How to Use Inspiration to Advance Your Leadership Journey

Inspiration is a dynamic force that moves you forward in your leadership path, not just a passing emotion. Your activities acquire purpose, resiliency, and steadfast determination as a result.

Set challenging objectives that complement your main sources of inspiration. Passion-driven goals are more likely to inspire and motivate you, especially under trying circumstances.

When faced with challenges, think back on your inspiration sources. Remind yourself of the initial motivations behind your travels. Your determination and attention may be rekindled by this recalibration.

Tell your group or community where you find inspiration. Your infectious passion might inspire a sense of purpose in the group.

Connecting with Your Leadership Purpose

Purpose, the underlying "why" that drives your leadership path, is at the core of inspiration. Making a connection to your leadership mission gives your actions a sense of importance and effect.

Consider the influence you want to have. What alteration or contribution do you hope to make? You are directed toward your goal by this reflection.

Your goals as a leader change as you gain experience and knowledge. Regularly evaluate how well your actions are in line with your goals.

Always make decisions and do actions with intention, making sure they are in line with your mission. Congruence between your purpose and your leadership style fosters trust and authenticity.

The fundamental connection between inspiration, passion, and purpose in leadership is celebrated in this chapter. Your leadership path gains authenticity and zeal by drawing on your sources of drive and passion. You advance by using inspiration as a driving force, maintaining your commitment even in the face of difficulties.

Your judgments and actions are profoundly anchored by your connection to your purpose as a leader. Your leadership is changed from a job to a calling—a goal motivated by passion and consistent with your core principles.

To inspire change and leave a lasting impression, leadership is about more than just completing goals. You become a light of transformation by identifying your sources of inspiration and connecting with your purpose. Your leadership journey develops into a symphony of fervor, purpose, and tremendous impact that motivates those around you to go out on their transformative journeys.

Chapter 10

Unearth Your Calling

Finding your calling is a crucial pursuit within the huge leadership environment. The central section of this chapter, "Unearth Your Calling," takes you on a trip into the depths of your interests, talents, and purpose. It focuses on the challenging process of identifying your leadership calling and the transformative impact of matching your leadership development with this profound feeling of purpose.

Discovering Your Hidden Talents and Passions

The first step in discovering your calling is to look within and discover your passions and natural talents. Your interests are the flames that ignite your soul, and your skills are how you may effect lasting change.

Think back to times when you were most involved and alive. These situations frequently highlight your passions—activities or causes that speak to your soul.

Recognize your abilities and qualities. You can transform your passions into meaningful acts by using your talents. Determine your areas of strength and your areas of delight.

Think about the pursuits that pass the hours by quickly because you are so absorbed in them. These situations frequently reveal your interests and skills.

Finding Your Special Purpose and Leadership Calling

While interests and skills stand alone as distinct threads, purpose joins them to create a meaningful whole. Aligning your interests and abilities with a more significant influence on the world is a necessary step in finding your mission and calling as a leader.

Think about the world change you want to bring about. What wrongdoings, difficulties, or changes connect strongly with you? This introspection frequently results in a sense of direction.

Think about the legacy you want to leave. What impact do you hope to have and how do you want to be remembered? You are guided toward your calling by this reflection.

The junction of what you love, what you are good at, and what the world needs is frequently where your calling lies. It is a location where your interests, skills, and purpose come together.

Your Leadership Journey and Your Calling Should Be Aligned

Your calling and your leadership path work together to produce a seamless dance of impact and authenticity. Your actions will be filled with passion, tenacity, and a profound sense of significance when your leadership is in alignment with your calling.

Make a vision for yourself that reflects your calling. Imagine the future you want and describe it in a way that encourages and inspires those around you.

Create a plan for your objectives and course of action based on your calling. Every choice, initiative, and encounter becomes an intentional step in the direction of achieving your goal.

Accept obstacles as chances to follow your calling. When you view difficulties as opportunities to change the world, they stop being obstacles and start becoming stepping stones on your path.

You learn what makes you come alive by discovering your passions and talents. Finding your special purpose and vocation enables you to bring these aspects into harmony with a wider influence, weaving a tapestry of tremendous meaning.

A commitment to lead with authenticity, passion, and purpose, alignment of your leadership journey with your calling is a transforming action. It catapults you out of the realm of traditional leadership and into one of deep influence and transformation.

Keep in mind that your calling serves as a beacon for you to follow even when you are hesitant. By matching your leadership path to your calling, you not only leave a lasting legacy but also encourage others to go out on their journeys of self-awareness and fulfillment. Your leadership develops into a symphony of interests, skills, and goals—a symphony that speaks to the hearts of those you lead and the world you hope to transform.

Chapter 11

The Importance of Learning for Exceptional Leaders

The quest for greatness in the always-changing field of leadership is founded on learning. The core of this chapter, "The Importance of Learning for Exceptional Leaders," explores the transforming potential of adopting a growth mindset. It looks at how lifelong learning may help build leaders, why it's important to push over mediocrity, and how to always improve personally and professionally.

Adopting A Growth Mindset When Leading

Outstanding leadership stems from a mindset that values development, learning, and adaptability. The idea that skills and intelligence can be improved through work, practice, and education is known as a growth mindset. Growth-minded leaders create resilience, thrive in the face of obstacles, and motivate their employees to achieve greater things.

Adopt a mindset that sees setbacks and failures as chances for growth and learning. Consider mistakes as stepping stones to improvement rather than something to be feared.

Encourage your team to have a culture of creativity and experimentation. Accept the notion that attempting novel strategies can be a worthwhile learning experience, even if they fail.

Set a good example. Share your personal growth and development experiences to show that you are committed to learning. This openness fosters an atmosphere where people are at ease taking chances and tackling new problems.

The Importance Of Lifelong Learning For The Development Of Leaders

Leadership is a dynamic journey rather than a set destination. The compass that directs this voyage is lifelong learning, which keeps leaders current, adaptive, and capable of handling the changing environment.

Set aside time just for studying. Invest in your ongoing improvement whether it be through formal education, reading, workshops, or online courses.

Keep an open mind and be curious. Explore areas outside of your primary area of expertise and look for diverse viewpoints. Your understanding is expanded, and your capacity for problem-solving is improved, thanks to this interdisciplinary approach.

Beyond acquiring technical skills, lifelong learning also includes developing one's emotional intelligence, communication skills, and leadership abilities. Spend time developing these soft talents because they are necessary for successful leadership.

Challenging Mediocrity Aiming for Greatness

Outstanding leaders strive for greatness rather than settling for mediocrity. This goal necessitates a dedication to ongoing development and a refusal to become complacent.

Set high expectations for you and your group. Make an effort to create a culture where excellence is the rule rather than the exception.

Continually assess your methods, plans, and results. Determine where there is room for progress and oppose the status quo. Encourage your staff to follow suit to promote an innovative culture.

Celebrate accomplishments, but also use them as launching pads for development. Use accomplishments as fuel to pursue even loftier objectives rather than resting on your laurels.

Techniques for Continual Professional and Personal Development

- The pursuit of continual improvement necessitates deliberate tactics that encourage development in all facets of your leadership journey.
- Create an individualized learning strategy. Set goals and specify the

activities you'll take to achieve them. Identify areas that need improvement.

- Ask for input from coworkers, mentors, and team members regularly. Constructive criticism offers perceptions that can direct your development.
- Connect with other businesspeople and leaders. Attend conferences, participate in activities hosted by the industry, and participate in conversations. You are exposed to fresh viewpoints and ideas through these exchanges.
- Make self-care a top priority to keep your mind sharp and perform at your best. For ongoing growth and

effectiveness, a healthy work-life balance is crucial.

Adopting a growth mindset encourages creativity and resiliency. Being a leader requires you to be flexible and relevant, which is ensured by lifelong learning. You are propelled beyond your comfort zone toward transformative influence when you challenge mediocrity and strive for excellence.

Continuous personal and professional progress is a principle that should underpin all of your decisions and actions. By committing to improvement, you not only strengthen your leadership skills but also motivate people around you to realize their full potential.

Keep in mind that leadership is about continually striving to improve yourself rather than about achieving a single goal. You not only lead with greatness when you embrace learning and growth, but you also leave behind a legacy of impact and inspiration. Your career as a leader becomes a symbol of the efficacy of ongoing development—a legacy that influences not just your life but also the lives of people you come into contact with.

Chapter 12

Empowering and Inspiring Others

The strands of empowerment and inspiration are carefully woven into the rich fabric of leadership. The heart of this chapter, "Empowering and Inspiring Others," delves into the art of delegation, the establishment of a culture of trust and collaboration, and the significant influence of inspiring and mentoring others to realize their hidden leadership potential.

Delegation and Empowerment

The ability to delegate effectively as a leader is critical to enabling your team to thrive. Delegation is more than just assigning work; it is a purposeful approach that allows individuals to provide their best efforts while also developing as leaders.

Determine each team member's abilities and interests. Assign tasks that are appropriate for their ability, to promote a sense of ownership and confidence.

Expectations and goals should be communicated clearly. Give guidelines while still allowing for autonomy and innovation. This equilibrium ensures that team members grasp the goal while also allowing them to thrive.

Encourage decision-making and issue-solving. Allow your employees to tackle problems independently, and provide guidance when necessary. As a result, people develop a sense of accountability and ownership.

Creating a Trust and Collaboration Culture

The underpinning of empowered teams is a culture of trust and collaboration. When there is trust, creativity flows, and communication and collaboration flourish.

Set an example. Give team members authority and support their decisions to demonstrate your faith in them. This establishes a culture of trust.

Encourage open dialogue. Create a climate in which team members may communicate their ideas, concerns, and opinions without fear of being judged.

Team achievements should be celebrated. Recognize that accomplishments are the result of a collaborative effort, and give credit to those who helped. This strengthens the sense of teamwork and solidarity.

Motivating And Mentoring Others To Reach Their Full Leadership Potential

Great leaders not only empower those they lead but also inspire and mentor them. Inspiring and mentoring others is a transforming experience that reveals untapped leadership potential while directing others onto their pathways of growth and impact.

Share your experience as a leader. Be honest about your difficulties, failures, and triumphs. This vulnerability humanizes your leadership and allows you to deliver relatable insights.

Recognize and develop talent. Look for hidden strengths and qualities in your team members. Encourage them to pursue possibilities for leadership and provide guidance along the way.

Provide constructive criticism. Provide feedback that highlights both your strengths and your opportunities for improvement. When handled with tact, constructive criticism promotes growth and improvement.

Delegation transforms into a tool for development, helping team members to reach their full potential. A culture of trust and collaboration promotes innovation and strengthens ties. Inspiring and mentoring team members not only awakens their leadership potential but also causes a beneficial ripple effect.

Remember that leadership is about uplifting others rather than elevating oneself. You leave a legacy of leadership by empowering and motivating others around you. Your leadership journey becomes a symphony of growth, mentorship, and impact—a symphony that resonates in the lives of others you've helped toward their untapped leadership potential.

Chapter 13

Leaving a Legacy

One of the most important concepts of leadership is sustaining your leadership legacy. This chapter looks into the essence of creating a lasting impression, the art of always growing and adapting your leadership style and the critical obligation of paying it forward by guaranteeing the growth of future leaders.

Leaving a Long-lasting Impression as a Leader

True leadership transcends tasks and titles, leaving an enduring effect on the people and environment it affects. Maintaining your leadership legacy entails instilling long-term change, cultivating a positive culture, and motivating others to carry on the torch.

Make an Impact Vision: A lasting legacy begins with a vision that is bigger than your physical presence. Consider the good changes you would like to see and the ideals you would like to instill.

Set an example: Your decisions and actions have an impact on your company or community. You establish an example for others to follow by continually living the ideas and beliefs you advocate.

Invest in Others: The success of the people you lead is inextricably linked to your legacy. Mentorship should be prioritized, as should opportunities for skill development and empowering others to assume leadership roles.

Evolving and Adapting Your Leadership Style

Leadership is a lifelong process. As the globe evolves, so should your strategy. To sustain your leadership legacy, you must be open to new ideas, willing to learn, and adaptable.

Consider and Apply: Examine your leadership strategies regularly. Consider what is functioning well, what may be improved, and where changes are needed.

Keep up to date: Keep a pulse on your industry or field. Keep up to date on new trends, technology, and best practices that may have an impact on your leadership style.

Seek comments from your team, colleagues, and mentors. Their viewpoints offer valuable perspectives that can help steer your development as a leader.

Paying It Forward: Developing Future Leaders

A true leadership legacy extends beyond your tenure and into the development of future leaders. Paying it forward entails developing emerging leaders and establishing a leadership development culture.

Recognize Potential: Individuals with a promise for leadership should be recognized. Encourage them to take on leadership responsibilities and offer them guidance to help them succeed.

Mentorship is Important: Mentor new leaders. Share your leadership experiences, insights, and challenges to assist others in their leadership journeys.

Create Opportunities for Growth: Give opportunities for skill development and advancement. Assign initiatives and duties that will help emerging leaders grow.

Maintaining your leadership legacy is not a passive effort; rather, it is a conscious commitment to growth, change, and the empowerment of others. Leaving a lasting impression necessitates authenticity, adaptability, and a never-ending commitment to sound change. You can ensure that your legacy remains relevant and impactful by constantly updating your leadership strategy. Furthermore, investing in the development of rising leaders ensures that your influence will be felt far into the future.

Remember that a leader's legacy is a living story of empowerment and transformation. You become a light of influence and effect by promoting growth in others and refining your leadership skills. Your leadership journey creates a symphony of inspiration, evolution, and lasting change—a symphony that shapes not only your legacy but also the collective story of leaders who carry your torch forward.

Conclusion

As we come to the end of our transformative trip through the pages of "Unleash Your Leadership Potential," we've dived deep into the heart of leadership, investigating the hidden qualities that distinguish exceptional leaders. We've excavated the essence of hidden leadership throughout this book, revealing the power within each individual to make a lasting difference.

This book has created a blueprint to unlock your hidden potential, from recognizing your intrinsic leadership skills to embracing your unique abilities. We've traveled through the terrains of effective communication, empathic leadership, and the art of overcoming obstacles, gaining significant insights into becoming a well-rounded and successful leader.

Remember that leadership is a manner of life, not a label. With the information you've gained here, you'll be able to negotiate the difficulties of leadership with honesty and confidence. Your journey toward realizing your leadership potential does not end here; it is a constant growth that you are now better prepared to undertake.

Allow the principles and teachings in this book to guide your behavior as you move forward. Lead with a growth mentality, inspire others with your words and actions, and help those around you thrive. Your leadership path is a woven tapestry of experiences, growth, and meaningful connections. Take advantage of this unique opportunity to leave a lasting legacy.

Finally, "Unleash Your Leadership Potential" is more than a book; it's an invitation to a lifelong path of leadership development. Carry forward the insight gained and continue to unlock your leadership potential as you turn the last page, creating a positive effect on your path and the lives of those you lead. Your leadership narrative is unique; let it shine brightly and encourage others to go on their leadership excellence journeys.